For my brothers,
whose interest sparked my own.

Contents

PURPOSE

I'm a casual fan of J. R. R. Tolkien's, *The Lord of the Rings* trilogy. By this, I mean that I have enjoyed the movies many times, slogged through some of the books, and have read bits of the *Silmarillion* - Tolkien's handbook for the lore surrounding his universe. The problem with being only a "casual" fan, is that my interest doesn't motivate me to do any in-depth study of the Tolkien-verse, and my relationship with the *Silmarillion* is flighty at best. That said, even without an encyclopedic knowledge of the *Silmarillion*, I still manage to get great enjoyment out of my experience with the base story of *The Lord of the Rings*. When I want to know more, I simply tune into my favorite Tolkien-based YouTube channel and get the cliff notes from those who have spent a lot more time in the material.

While my interest in Tolkien may be casual, my interest in the Bible is professional. The Book of Enoch (or 1 Enoch) can be described as containing the "lore" that surrounds the beliefs of the prominent characters of the Bible, and I put together *Luminary* for the purpose of giving the "YouTube video," cliff-note version of the book of Enoch.

If you've ever read the books of Isaiah or Jeremiah, or any of the longer works in the Bible, you'll know that they are long, drawn out, and rich with chapter upon chapter of spiritual meat. While they are very enriching, they are also very long. For reference, Isaiah clocks in at 66 chapters.

The Book of Enoch has 105 chapters. Enter *Luminary*.

This is, admittedly, a work of errors. The concepts, ideas, and classifications expressed in these pages without a doubt contain a number of inaccuracies based on faulty assumptions and incomplete historical data. While these weaknesses could not be helped, every attempt has been made at a broad, holistic understanding of the things presented. The Book of 1 Enoch is a work that was widely respected, referenced, and quoted by several of the Old and New Testament authors. The exact timing and authorship of each of the sections is not known, but regardless of this it seems clear that at least some of the New Testament writers regarded its work to be at least partially authoritative. It is with this assumption in mind that this work was created. Its purpose is to present a concise road map of some of the "givens" that those in the second-temple period through the early church period held. These beliefs include language referring to the afterlife, the organizational system of heavenly beings and locations, and the origin of certain cultural developments. Descriptions that are intriguing at least, and very helpful at most.

This book is meant to serve as a quick reference guide for understanding broad themes at-a-glance, with additional information provided for those who desire more information. In general, each section will consist of a broad header, with specific names listed in large bold letters. Beneath the names will list some bullet points of general facts for at-a-glance reference. Beneath these bullets will be a summation of what information we have concerning the subject, with additional references beneath it all in subtext. These additional references will be a mixture of Biblical references to the subjects, as well as my personal thoughts on some of the more confusing items.

As I put this work together, I have made every effort to present the ideas in a way that is, to the best of my understanding, faithful to the original context and beliefs of the Second-Temple Jews through the time of the early church writings. While I personally find an abundance of helpful information for understanding the Scriptures, it should be clearly understood that not every statement aligns to my personal beliefs regarding the spiritual realm, its prominent characters, or the afterlife. The contents of *Luminary* will be presented as fact inasmuch as it seeks to be an accurate presentation of a set of ancient beliefs, rather than how this author believes the cosmos to accurately function.

The Book of Enoch, as with any ancient literature, presents certain challenges in presentation to modern readers. This work makes no attempt to unpack every literary style found within the pages of 1 Enoch, but rather seeks to simplify and condense the raw information presented. The mature Christian should read with wisdom, pursuing a greater understanding of the Scriptures and the context into which the Savior walked. These things may vary in historical accuracy, but their relevance is upheld by the importance of those who were so familiar with its themes. Enjoy if the following pages lead you into further love of Jesus and His Word, or discard if they don't.

Be blessed. Let's begin.

LUMINARY

"Behold, the Lord comes with ten thousands of His holy ones..."

Jude, the brother of Jesus

Part 1: The Watchers

"I saw in the visions of my head as I lay in bed,
and behold, a watcher, a holy one,
came down from heaven."

Nebuchadnezzar, King of Babylon

INTRODUCTION TO THE WATCHERS

"For we do not wrestle against flesh and blood, but against the rulers, against the authorities, against the cosmic powers over this present darkness, against the spiritual forces of evil in the heavenly places."

Paul, the Apostle

To say that the terms "Watcher" and "Angel" are essentially interchangeable is partially true, as a faithful, heavenly servant of God is called a "Watcher" in the book of Daniel[1]. However, the term "Watcher" technically applies to a classification of angel that is tasked with observing and interceding for mankind. That said, in this and most other works, the term "Watcher" will generally refer to the 200 angels that descended to take human women for themselves at the beginning of Genesis 6 - an event that this work will refer to as the "Incursion."

Watchers have all the major characteristics of the angelic figures that appear throughout the Scriptures. While they are primarily spiritual beings, they have the ability to manifest in the physical world in various forms, including human.

Watchers were once obedient angels who fell under the influence of one or more of their members post-creation and chose to come and breed

1 - Daniel 4:7

with human women. This would be a separate angelic "Fall" than that which involved rebel angels who act still today, though some characters will overlap in the narratives. For the most part, the present-day distinction between Watchers and Fallen Angels exists in the fact that the Watchers of old would currently be imprisoned until the Great Judgment, while the Fallen Angels are still free to exercise some authority on earth.

The chief crimes of the Watchers included their incursion on earth and the theft of divine secrets that had been held in heaven in reserve. These secrets were intended to have been dispersed to humanity over time, likely climaxing in the arrival of Jesus, but their theft and early dispersion among humanity added to the charges against the Watchers.

Apparently, the Watchers were either 1) allowed to continue their actions for a brief time after the Great Flood, or 2) there were at least two Incursion events. This is evidenced by 1) the claim in Genesis 6 that the Nephilim were present *after* the flood[2], 2) the claim of the Israelite spies in Numbers 13, and 3) the presence of Goliath - a Nephilim descendant - and his kin found at various times in the land of Canaan.

Watchers were ultimately punished and kept in a variety of prisons. These prisons are located within the spiritual dimension, though some have geographical locations associated with them as well, as we will see.

2 - In some circles there exists a debate over the global vs. local-nature of the Great Flood of Noah. If the Great Flood was merely a localized event, then there was likely only one group of Watchers. Conversely, if the Great Flood was a global event, then there would have naturally had to have been multiple incursions by the Watchers.

THEFTS OF THE WATCHERS

Names of Prominent Watchers

- Semjaza
- Kokab(l)el
- Ezeqeel
- Baraqijal
- Armaros
- Sariel
- Araqiel
- Azazel
- Shamsiel

Summary

During their interactions with humanity, some of the Watchers were said to have brought secrets to mankind that they "stole" from heaven. These secrets were thought valuable by the Watchers[3], but were later revealed to be some of the lesser knowledge that heaven had to offer[4]. Though other Watchers were named in the narrative, they had little to contribute[5].

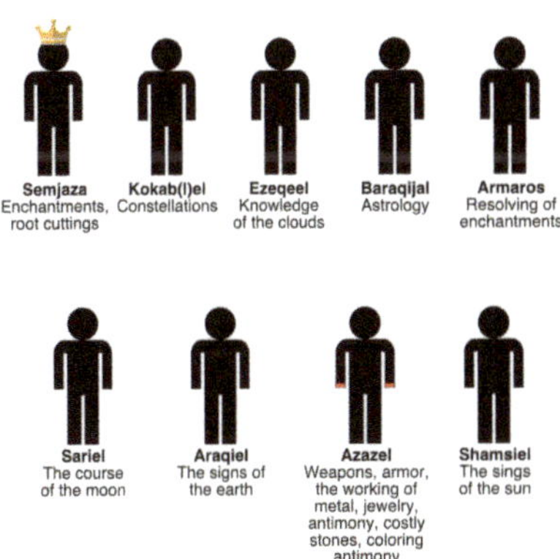

3 - Sorcery, witchcraft, making molten images, silver from the dust of the earth, and how soft metal originates in the earth

4 - Enoch 16:3, 1 Peter 1:10-12

5 - Samlazaz, Araklba, Rameel, Danel, Asael, Batarel, Ananel, Zaqiel, Samsapeel, Satarel, Turel, and Jomjael

Azazel

"Aaron shall offer the bull as a sin offering for himself and shall make atonement for himself and for his house. Then he shall take the two goats and set them before the Lord at the entrance of the tent of meeting. And Aaron shall cast lots over the two goats, one lot for the Lord and the other lot for Azazel. And Aaron shall present the goat on which the lot fell for the Lord and use it as a sin offering, but the goat on which the lot fell for Azazel shall be presented alive before the Lord to make atonement over it, that it may be sent away into the wilderness to Azazel."

Excerpt from the Levitical Law of Moses

Key Themes

- Taught humans how to make armor and weapons, and how to work metals
- Introduced jewelry, makeup, and coloring tinctures
- The one to whom the Jewish scapegoat was dedicated to during Yom Kippur
- Ascribed "all sin"
- Credited with teaching unrighteousness to humanity and revealing eternal secrets which men had tried to learn but had been preserved in heaven
- Was put in chains and imprisoned underground in Dudael

Summary

Azazel is probably the most interesting Watcher in the Book of Enoch. He was originally listed as a lesser chief among the 200, subservient to Semjaza. However, his thefts and misconducts were damning enough that he received unique mention and punishment among the other Watchers.

Azazel had the distinction of being the one to introduce the working of metals and the forging of weapons of war (knives, swords, shields, and breastplates). He introduced bracelets, ornaments, antimony (used in ancient times for medicine and cosmetics), beautifying of the eyelids, costly stones, and coloring tinctures. The negative effects of the early introduction of these elements into humanity caused him to receive the designation of being ascribed, “all sin” by God. He was credited with teaching unrighteousness to humanity and revealing eternal secrets which men had tried to learn, but had been preserved in heaven.

In light of this, Azazel was put in chains and imprisoned underground in Dudael - a land east of Jerusalem[6].

Biblical Reference

Azazel also has the distinction of being the only Watcher to be mentioned by name in the Old Testament. Each year on the Day of Atonement, the ancient Jews were instructed in Leviticus 16 to present two scapegoats to take on the sins of God’s people. One was to be sacrificed, and the other was to be released in the wilderness, east of Jerusalem, “to Azazel.”

6 - 2 Peter 2:4

SATAN

"But when the archangel Michael, contending with the devil, was disputing about the body of Moses, he did not presume to pronounce a blasphemous judgment, but said, 'The Lord rebuke you.'"

Jude, the brother of Jesus

Key Themes

- Has instruments prepared for the kings and mighty men to kill each other with
- Subjects the watchers and leads astray those who dwell on the earth

Summary

Satan, while not listed as a Watcher, bears mentioning because of the closeness of his affiliation with Azazel. The Book of Enoch is divided into five sections, the second of which is known as "The Parables." In it, we are given a new list of Watchers and their misdeeds, and are briefly presented with the character, Satan. Similar to Azazel, Satan is credited with instructing fallen angels to prepare instruments for the kings and mighty men of the world to kill each other with. It is later said that Satan "subjects the Watchers and leads astray those who dwell on the earth."

Because of the parabolic nature of the second section of First Enoch, the closeness of the descriptions of Satan and some of the other Watchers is worth noting.

JEQON

Key Themes

- The one who led astray the sons of God (Watchers), brought them down to earth, and led them astray through the daughters of men

ASBEEL

Key Themes

- Imparted to the Watchers evil counsel and led them astray so that they defiled their bodies with the women

SEMJAZA - CHIEF OF THE WATCHERS

Key Themes

- Taught enchantments and root cuttings
- Given authority to bear rule over his associates
- Judged in the burning Valley
- Leader of the Watchers, initiated the pact

Who Started It?

Semjaza was the one that God delegated authority over the Watchers. It was he that gave the final approval for the Incursion, and it was he that created the pact that all the other Watchers agreed to. Semjaza was nervous that if he stepped forward on his own, that all the other Watchers would back out at the last moment and leave him to fend for himself. Because of this, he created a pact that the 200 Watchers would all agree to carry out the fullness of the act along with him.

Though Semjaza was the leader of the Watchers, he wasn't the one who originated the idea for the incursion. The idea actually originated from two Watchers named Asbeel and Jeqon. It was through their counsel that the Watchers (the "sons of God") were led astray to defile their bodies with the human women.

GADREEL

Key Themes

- Showed the children of men all the blows of death
- Led astray Eve
- Showed humans weapons of death like the shield and coat of mail, battle sword, and others

Summary

Gadreel is another interesting figure, because of the similarities between him, Azazel, and the classical portrayal of Satan. Similar to Azazel, the Book of Enoch similarly attributes him the act of showing the children of men all the blows of death, and weapons like the shield, coat of mail, battle sword, and others. Most interesting however, is that Gadreel is credited as being the identity of the serpent who lead astray Eve in the Garden of Eden.

PNENUME

Key Themes

- Taught the children of men the bitter and the sweet,
- Taught them all the secrets of their wisdom,
- Instructed mankind in writing with ink and paper

ASBEEL

Key Themes

- Showed humans the wicked smiting of spirits and demons, smiting of the embryo in the womb, the smiting of the bites of the serpent, the smiting through the noontide heat
- The son of the serpent, named Taba'et

Summary

There are other Watchers named[7], but two more are worth mentioning.

Pnenume was attributed with teaching mankind a great, though mostly unlisted, volume of secrets that the Watchers brought from heaven. The text also gives special mention to the fact that Pnenume instructed mankind in writing with ink and paper and the signing of contracts. A trivial contribution by some estimations, but it was this contribution that Enoch records a sobering observation: that mankind was created to act in good faith towards their neighbor, but in this breach of trust allowed for the perpetuation of sin for eternity.

7 - Named Artaqifa, Armen, Kokabel, Rumjal, Danjal, Neqael, Baraqel, Batarjal, Busasejal, Hananel, Turael, Jetrel, Tumael, Rumael, Simapesiel

THE NEPHILIM

"The Nephilim were on the earth in those days, and also afterward, when the sons of God came in to the daughters of man and they bore children to them. These were the mighty men who were of old, the men of renown."

Moses and Enoch, the Prophets

Key Themes

- Direct offspring of Watchers and human women,
- Each was three-thousand ells tall[8]
- Called "evil spirits" after their bodies were destroyed

Summary

The Nephilim and their effects play a prominent role in the Biblical accounts. These were direct descendants of the Watchers and human women. Almost every ancient account of early human civilization has a reference to these half-man, half-heavenly hybrids. According to the Book of Enoch, the first-generation Nephilim were enormous - literally mountains of men. Their estimated size were 3,000 ells (2.13 miles) tall. Whether this measurement was literal or hyperbolic to describe their enormous stature, we are told that the land could not support enough food[9] for them. With each generation, they apparently got

8 - or 2.13 miles

9 - Note the apparent size of the fruit the Israelites brought back from their scouting mission in Numbers 13

progressively smaller, as several generations later we find them occupying Canaan - a land that could support enough food - and a description of a still massive, though notably smaller description. Their noted size decreases again a few generations later with the description of Goliath and his brothers being closer to 10 feet tall.

When the Nephilim died, their hybrid spirits - born of heaven and earth but belonging to neither - persisted on earth as Evil Spirits.

Evil Spirits

"When Jesus had stepped out on land, there met him a man from the city who had demons. For a long time he had worn no clothes, and he had not lived in a house but among the tombs. When he saw Jesus, he cried out and fell down before him and said with a loud voice, "What have you to do with me, Jesus, Son of the Most High God? I beg you, do not torment me." For He had commanded the unclean spirit to come out of the man... Jesus then asked him, "What is your name?" And he said, "Legion," for many demons had entered him. And they begged him not to command them to depart into the abyss."

Luke, the Physician

Key Themes

- Afflict, oppress, destroy, attack, do battle, and work destruction on the earth and cause trouble
- Hunger and thirst without being able to eat or drink
- Cause offenses
- Will destroy without incurring judgment until the day of the consummation
- May assume several forms
- Lead humanity astray into sacrificing to demons as gods

Summary

After the Nephilim died, their spirits persisted on earth as Evil Spirits. They experienced the sensations of hunger and thirst, but were never able to eat or drink. They afflict, oppress, destroy, attack, do battle, and work destruction on the earth and cause general trouble for humanity. They have a working knowledge of things going on in both the spiritual and physical dimensions, and will persist until the Great Judgment where they will be removed from humanity forever.

Jesus' ministry on earth had a great deal to do with diminishing the effects of these creatures. It is this spiritual blight that Scripture refers to when talking about demons and evil spirits. This classification of spiritual enemy would be entirely separate from and inferior to the principalities aligned against God's people mentioned elsewhere in the New Testament, and lack the power, authority, and guile of fallen, hostile angels.

IMPLICATIONS OF THE WATCHERS

For centuries, Western doctrinal thought has existed on its own without the incorporation of the ideas presented in the Book of Enoch. Yet space should be made for a wholistic understanding of the context in which the Scriptures were written. Understanding this, it serves the student of the Scriptures to parcel out the implications of some of the ideas presented in the texts orbiting the Bible it its day.

It's possible that the ideas expressed in the Book of Enoch are more or less what we could call "literal" in how the reader was originally to understand them. Because many scholars consider ancient Semitic writings to have varying degrees of historically "accurate" depictions of events as we would understand historic accuracy, it becomes difficult to give every angle on every possible interpretation of the Book of Enoch - especially since it hasn't been subjected to the amount of scrutiny that the canonical books have.

For the sake of linear thinking, let us imagine that most of the characters, creatures, and events in the Book of Enoch are largely literal - meaning that they actually existed in a way that corresponds with how they are presented in the text.

The Accuser

Few Biblical scholars seem to question the events of the Incursion as it relates to the creation of the Nephilim. Yet if the different named Watchers committed acts in accordance to the text, then it forces the reader to consider the nature of the hostile spirits in the world, particularly that of Satan. You will notice that some of the acts traditionally attributed to a single leader of the enemy spiritual forces are split into at least three different personalities - namely Azazel, Gadreel, and Satan. Taking into account that "Satan" is technically a classification meaning "Accuser," it is not outside the realm of possibility that the Edenic snake that tempted Eve (here, Gadreel) may be a different being than the one who is attributed all evil (here, Azazel). If this distinction exists, "Satan" would then refer more to the line of spiritual beings who would defy their created order, rather than a singular leader across all time. This would not necessarily contradict God's denouement of the snake in Genesis 3, and would fall in line with some of the other texts found in the Book of Enoch. Strictly speaking, neither the name "Lucifer," nor the occurrence of his failed attempt to overthrow heaven exists within the Biblical texts.

Based on the treatment of Azazel in Leviticus 16, it seems as though being bound beneath the desert floor may not remove the Watchers entirely from the happenings on earth in their general vicinity.

Nephilim

The existence of Nephilim goes beyond ancient Jewish writings, and is incorporated into almost every ancient historical account. Whereas pagan cultures credit the gods with the siring of powerful demigods who accomplished amazing feats and ruled cities, Jewish belief acknowledged the existence of these beings and attributed their existence to a perversion of the divine order.

Demons

Traditional thought attributes the term "demon" to the fallen angels that fell with Satan, who are relatively equal in stature to regular angels. The Book of Enoch demotes demons to be the spirits of the dead half-breed race of Nephilim. These spirits were said to roam the earth and cause trouble, as well as having certain negative effects on human physiology and psychology.

PART 2: THE ANGELS

"Do not neglect to show hospitality to strangers, for thereby some have entertained angels unawares."

Paul, the Apostle

Angel Classes

• **Archangel**: seven distinctly prominent angels who are set over large portions of creation[10]

• **Seraphim**: bless the Lord forever around His throne[11]

• **Cherubim**: bring messages from God to humanity[12]

• **Ophanim**: those who "sleep not and guard the Throne of His glory"[13]

• **Watchers**: those originally charged with maintaining records of humanity, as well as interceding between God and mankind

Summary

Based on what we can discern from the Bible and the Book of Enoch, there seem to be no fewer than four types (or classes) of angel, in addition to the seven archangels.

10 - 1 Thessalonians 4:16, Daniel 10:12, Jude 1:9

11 - Isaiah 6:2, Revelation 4:8

12 - Ezekiel 1:5-11

13 - Enoch 70

The Seven Archangels

"When the Lamb opened the seventh seal, there was silence in heaven for about half an hour. Then I saw the seven angels who stand before God, and seven trumpets were given to them."

John, the Apostle

Names of the Archangels

Uriel	Remiel
Michael	Saraqael
Raphael	Raguel
Gabriel	

The best we can discern, the angelic forces of heaven are divided into divisions, with leaders over various members of their numbers. We get an idea of some of the divisions, with groupings of 10, 50, and 100 listed in the Book of Enoch. Beings known as archangels generally govern larger bodies of space and interact with lower functionaries when necessary.

Biblical References

The book of Revelation references "the seven angels who stand before God." The use of the article "the" indicates that these seven were a concept that was already familiar with the readers of this early church work. The Book of Enoch assigns names and functions to each of these seven angels.

URIEL

Key Themes

- Over the world and Tartarus
- Identity of the angel who Spoke to Noah
- Guide to the Prisons and the "Blessed/Cursed Places"
- Archangel whom God has set forever over all the luminaries of the heaven, in the heaven, and in the world[14]
- Has the power over night and day in the heaven to cause the light to give light to men

Summary

Uriel is a prominent character in the Book of Enoch and spends much of the time as the author's companion through the cosmos. He is named as the angel who conversed with Noah about the coming of the Great Flood, and his primary function is to exercise authority over the sun, moon, stars, and various other spacial entities.

14 - i.e. the sun, moon, and stars, and "all the ministering creatures which make their revolution in all the chariots of the heaven"

MICHAEL

"But I will tell you what is inscribed in the book of truth: there is none who contends by my side against these except Michael, your prince."

"At that time shall arise Michael, the great prince who has charge of your people..."

Daniel, the Prophet

Key Themes

- Blesses God forever
- Merciful and patient
- Set over the best part of mankind and over chaos
- Binds the hosts of Azazel and casts them into the burning furnace
- Took up the distress call of the humans
- Assisted Uriel in eliminating the children of the Watchers
- Charged with binding Semjaza and the other Watchers in the valleys of the earth

Summary

Michael is referenced frequently in the Bible and the Book of Enoch. He is distinct in that his character traits are mentioned as being merciful and patient. He has been given charge over God's people throughout time, and has often been given some of the more militant tasks - including binding the hosts of Azazel and Semjaza, eliminating the children of the Watchers (Nephilim), contending with the devil[15], battling hostile angels[16], and is traditionally attributed with binding the devil in the Lake of Fire[17], though his name is not specifically mentioned for this particular feat.

15 - Jude 9
16 - Daniel 10:13
17 - Revelation 20:1-3

GABRIEL

"I heard a man's voice between the banks of the Ulai, and it called, 'Gabriel, make this man understand the vision.' So he came near where I stood. And when he came, I was frightened and fell on my face."

Daniel, the Prophet

Key Themes

- Charged to kill all of the children of the Watchers by causing them to kill each other off
- Set over Paradise (the "Blessed Place"), the serpents, and the Cherubim

Summary

Gabriel is most well-known as being the angel who delivered the interpretation of a dream to Daniel, and to Mary the news about Christ. He does, however, have a much broader set of responsibilities in the Book of Enoch. His first responsibility given was to kill all of the children of the Watchers (Nephilim) by causing them to kill each other off. While we are not given an exact account of the destruction of the Nephilim, it is interesting to note that the few remaining ones left alive by the time of David were all men of war.

Gabriel was also set over the "Blessed Place"[18] or "Paradise,"[19] as well as the Cherubim. There is a note about him being set over the "serpents," though no further explanation is given and likely was more clear to the original readers.

18 -Enoch 27, Matthew 5:7

19 - Luke 23:43

Raphael

"And the angels who did not stay within their own position of authority, but left their proper dwelling, he has kept in eternal chains under gloomy darkness until the judgment of the great day"

Jude, the Brother of Jesus

Key Themes

- Ordered to bind Azazel in the desert in Dudael
- Takes vengeance on the world of the luminaries
- Blesses Jesus and His elect
- Set over all diseases and human wounds
- Binds the hosts of Azazel and casts them into the burning furnace

Summary

Raphael is never mentioned in the Bible explicitly, though his presence is likely assumed in Revelation when it references the seven angels surrounding the throne. He (along with Michael, Gabriel, and Phanuel) was ordered to bind Azazel in the desert in Dudael[20], which is a desert region to the east of Jerusalem.

His general responsibilities include taking vengeance on the "world of the luminaries" - meaning the stars, moons, and planets. He is also the angel who guided Enoch through the "Hollow Places," as well as the features of Eden. After the Eden Fall, he was set over all diseases and human wounds.

20 - 2 Peter 2:4

Remiel

Key Theme

- Set over those who rise

Summary

Little is known about this archangel, as instances of humans "rising," presumably from death, are a rarity in the Bible. One notable instance is that following the death of Christ there were several dead that were raised[21], among several other abnormalities.

Saraqael

Key Theme

- Set over the spirits who sin in the spirit

Summary

The primary reference we have for spirits who "sin in the spirit" can be found in the book of Daniel[22] where we have the clearest description of hostile spirits acting in opposition to those in obedience to God. Saraqael would then be the archangel responsible for managing those (and possibly other) spirits who would act in defiance of the divine order.

21 - Matthew 27:52-53

22 - Daniel 10:13

RAGUEL

Key Theme

• Takes vengeance on the world of the luminaries

Summary

If there was little known about Raphael, there is even less about Raguel. Generally in the Book of Enoch, "the world of the luminaries" refers to the stars and other heavenly bodies, rather than referring to angelic beings.

Lower Angels

Zotiel

"He drove out the man, and at the east of the garden of Eden he placed the cherubim and a flaming sword that turned every way to guard the way to the tree of life."

Moses, the Prophet

Key Theme

- Name of the angel guarding Eden

Summary

According to the Book of Enoch, this is the name of the angel placed at the entrance to the Garden of Eden, apparently still there during the time of Enoch.

KASBEEL

Key Themes

- Requested chief of the oath he showed to the holy ones
- Once lived “High above in glory”
- Biqa
- Akae
- Requested Michael to show him the hidden name "that he might enunciate it in the oath, so that those might quake before that name and oath who revealed all that was in secret to the children of men"

Summary

Kasbeel is an interesting character, as the details are as vague as they are intriguing. He is certainly considered in the text to be one of the “good,” unfallen angels, and is possibly the name of the angel who would be tasked with proclaiming the greatness of the Son of Man to the angels in captivity[23].

Kasbeel apparently asked for permission to proclaim an “oath” to the captive Watchers, and later handed over the “oath” to Michael. The oath is described in Enoch 69:16-29 and describes the Source of the power by Which the universe continues on its course and by Which it all holds together. This Source is revealed in Colossians 1:16-17 to be Jesus - named the Son of Man in Enoch 69.

Kasbeel only appears in the book of the Parables, so it is possible that his existence is less literal in nature, and rather points forward to the Son of Man’s proclamation of victory, eventually fully realized by Peter[24].

23 - 1 Peter 3:19-22

24 - 1 Peter 3:22

PHANUEL

Key Themes

- Fends off devils, forbidding them to come before God to accuse humans
- Set over the repentance unto hope of those who inherit eternal life
- Binds the hosts of Azazel and casts them into the burning furnace

Summary

In the Bible, there are several references to the Accuser (Satan) that comes before God in an attempt to sway His favor against humanity because of their sins. The forces of Satan would overrun the heavenly courtroom with their accusations if they could, but it is the job of Phanuel and the other Ophanim to stop incursions like that from happening out of turn. Phanuel's role is that of advocate for the elect, and plays both spiritually offensive and defensive roles for humanity's sake.

Implications of The Angels

The implications surrounding the Book of Enoch's presentation of the seven archangels are few and have more to do with spiritual "world building" than doctrinal formation. However, Saraqael's responsibility over the "spirits who sin in the spirit" may give some insight into passages such as Daniel 10, where the angelic beings set over particular geographical locations apparently need to be routinely brought under submission. This concept seems to hint towards a higher degree of angelic autonomy, with angels having a greater ability to step out of (and, it follows, come back into) obedience than is traditionally assumed.

Similarly, it's interesting to see how the Fall seems to have corrupted even the stars, planets, and other heavenly fixtures. Multiple archangels are dedicated to dealing with the heavenly bodies that do not function as they were originally intended. Apparently, it was not just earth that was affected by the Fall, but all of creation.

Memorandum 1: Creatures & Sirens

LEVIATHAN

In that day the Lord with His hard and great and strong sword will punish Leviathan the fleeing serpent, Leviathan the twisting serpent, and He will slay the dragon that is in the sea.

Isaiah, the Prophet

Key Themes

- Female
- Dwells in the abysses of the ocean over the fountains of the waters

Summary

Leviathan is pictured in Scripture as a violent sea monster armed with almost indestructible, tightly-knit scales and the ability to breathe fire[25]. In the book of Enoch, she is created as the sea-based counter to Behemoth.

25 - Job 41

BEHEMOTH

He is the foremost of God's works; only his Maker can draw the sword against him.

The Author of the Book of Job

Key Themes

• Male
• Occupied the waste wilderness of Duidain on the east of the Garden

Summary

Behemoth is an imposing figure that was said to roam the deserts of Duidain - the same region under which Azazel was said to have been imprisoned. He is the land-based counterpart to Leviathan and has no equal in stature on the surface of the earth.

SIRENS

"That is why a wife ought to have a symbol of authority on her head, because of the angels."

Paul, the Apostle

Key Themes

- Daughters of Cain who were striking in beauty and were associated with evil and singing - possibly in mourning of what had become of them[26]
- The women who slept with the Watchers

Summary

"Siren" is a term that appears in Greek and ancient Jewish literature that, here, refers to the original group of women who gave birth to the original set of Nephilim. The term is not mentioned in 1 Enoch or the Bible, and can only be found in the Zohar - a significantly less reliable work, more within the genre of Jewish legend than anything else. While the Zohar gives a more eternal purpose of these women, there is little else to suggest what happened to these women post-Incursion, though the term is helpful to use in reference for the sake of tedium.

26 - The Zohar

Part 3: Purgatories and Prisons

"And I saw the dead, great and small, standing before the throne, and books were opened. Then another book was opened, which is the book of life. And the dead were judged by what was written in the books, according to what they had done. And the sea gave up the dead who were in it, Death and Hades gave up the dead who were in them, and they were judged, each one of them, according to what they had done."

John, the Apostle

Introduction to The Purgatories & Prisons

The descriptions of the "Purgatories and Prisons" in the spiritual realm are of particular interest when trying to understand the way that the people of Jesus' day understood the afterlife. Many modern traditions make an attempt to simplify these into generalized statements about "heaven" and "hell," but the ancient Jews had a much more robust view towards the afterlife.

It is interesting to note that Jesus rarely, if ever, spent any recorded effort in correcting these belief systems, usually reserving corrective statements regarding the afterlife for misunderstandings in the people's experience within them, as he did to the Sadducees in Mark 12.

While it would not be technically incorrect to make some sweeping generalizations to these eternal resting places, it does a disservice to several concepts revealed not only in ancient non-canonical literature, but also those found in the Bible to do so.

Having a general understanding of these various spiritual holding places will hopefully serve to illuminate the broader context of what may otherwise seem to be vague passages in Scripture.

PRISON #1

"For Christ also suffered once for sins, the righteous for the unrighteous, that he might bring us to God, being put to death in the flesh but made alive in the spirit, in which he went and proclaimed to the spirits in prison, because they formerly did not obey, when God's patience waited in the days of Noah, while the ark was being prepared."

Peter, the Apostle

Key Themes

- Has no firmament of heaven above, and no firm ground beneath it, no water, no birds
- A waste and horrible place
- Not originally designed to be a prison, but a place between the heavens and earth
- A prison for the "stars and the host of heaven"
- Prison for the angels who connected themselves with women and their spirits who lead humans astray into sacrificing to demons as gods
- Holds the number of starts that have transgressed the commandment of the Lord for 10,000 years

Summary

With the advent of fallen angels, there became a necessity for a holding place for those angels who transgressed in the days of Noah. Some, like Azazel, were kept in special spiritual prisons that were tied to a particular geographic region. Most, however, were imprisoned in a dimension that was neither tied to the heavens, nor to the earth, but rather existed in a spiritual wasteland separate from the two.

It was this wasteland that the evil spirits within the Legion begged Jesus not to cast them into. It was for good reason that they should fear it, for there is nothing within this plane of existence. There were no creatures, no sky, and no ground. This prison would hold most of the Watchers for 10,000 years - the "time entailed by their sins."[27]

27 - if this period of time is a literal sentence with earth-based years, then their release would happen sometime close to the year 7,630 A.D.

PRISON #2

"For if God did not spare angels when they sinned, but cast them into hell and committed them to chains of gloomy darkness to be kept until the judgment; if he did not spare the ancient world, but preserved Noah, a herald of righteousness, with seven others, when he brought a flood upon the world of the ungodly... then the Lord knows how to rescue the godly from trials, and to keep the unrighteous under punishment until the day of judgment, and especially those who indulge in the lust of defiling passion and despise authority."

Peter, the Apostle

Key Themes

- Full of great descending columns of fire, too big to take in the full size.
- Also called "hell" or "the Lake of Fire"[28]
- The forever prison of the angels[29]

Summary

The second prison of the angels is known in Scripture as the Lake of Fire. This is the eternal prison that Satan and his followers will be cast into for all eternity.

28 - 2 Peter 2:4
29 - Revelation 20:10, Matthew 25:41

INTRODUCTION TO HOLLOW PLACES

"The poor man died and was carried by the angels to Abraham's side. The rich man also died and was buried, and in Hades, being in torment, he lifted up his eyes and saw Abraham far off and Lazarus at his side. And he called out, 'Father Abraham, have mercy on me, and send Lazarus to dip the end of his finger in water and cool my tongue, for I am in anguish in this flame.' But Abraham said, 'Child, remember that you in your lifetime received your good things, and Lazarus in like manner bad things; but now he is comforted here, and you are in anguish. And besides all this, between us and you a great chasm has been fixed, in order that those who would pass from here to you may not be able, and none may cross from there to us.'"

Jesus

Key Theme

• Created "that the spirits of the dead should assemble therein" until the Great Judgment

Summary

Scripture makes some references to "Death" and "Hades" and various states of rest or unrest after the humans die. The most prominent reference to this is the temporary interruption of the prophet Samuel's rest by Saul and the Witch of Endor. The Book of Enoch separates these various Hollow Places in the cosmos into four groups - each of which containing souls existing in varying conditions based on the nature of their life.

It's interesting to note that these places were not originally intended to hold human souls, as humans were never to have died. After the Fall in Eden, these Hollow Places were then retrofitted to be a holding ground until the Great Judgment.

The End of the Hollow Places

While some of the descriptions are more or less vague, we know from the Apostle John's account in Revelation that once Jesus reigns on earth, these places will be done away with[30] and thrown into the Lake of Fire.

30 - Revelation 20:14

Hollow Place #1

The woman said to him, "Surely you know what Saul has done, how he has cut off the mediums and the necromancers from the land. ... Whom shall I bring up for you?" He said, "Bring up Samuel for me." ...Then Samuel said to Saul, "Why have you disturbed me by bringing me up?"

Gad, the Seer

Key Themes

- Created for the spirits of the righteous
- Has a large spring of water

Summary

The first of the Hollow Places is the closest to what most people think of when they think of "heaven." This is where the spirits of the righteous wait in blissful rest until the Great Judgment.

Hollow Place #2

"Many of those who sleep in the dust of the earth will awake, some to eternal life, and some to shame and eternal contempt."

Daniel, the Prophet

Key Themes

- Made for sinners when they die and judgment has not been executed on them in their lifetime.
- Very painful

Summary

It is in this Hollow Place that the majority of human souls would find their way to after death. Those who were (pre-death of Jesus) less than righteous but not complete in transgression would wait here to be judged by Christ in the Great Judgment.

Hollow Place #3

Key Theme

- Made for those who "make their suit [and] make disclosures concerning their destruction in the days of the sinners."

Summary

In some cases, there may be an instance where those who died (pre-death of Jesus) may have believed themselves to have suffered unjustly in their lifetime. These would likely await the Great Judgment for the Son of Man to plead their case.

HOLLOW PLACE #4

Key Themes

- Made for those who were not righteous but sinners - complete in transgression
- Their spirits will not be slain in the day of judgment nor will they be raised from there

Summary

This is the final resting place for those who died undoubtedly as sinners. This place has the unique distinction of being eternal among the Hollow Places - meaning that while other human spirits may be annihilated in the Great Judgment, these select individuals would remain imprisoned in this place for eternity.

Fiery Mountain Range

Key Themes

- A mountain range of 7 "mountains of fire" arranged in a circle with 1 of them in the center which is taller than the rest and shaped like a throne - this is God's throne for when He resides on earth after the Great Judgment
- The center throne is surrounded by trees, among which there is one especially desirable, "fragrant" tree
- The "Fragrant Tree" will be transplanted to the holy place after the Great Judgment and God's people will eat of it and live very long lives

Summary

The Fiery Mountain Range is a series of 7 mountains, each made of different kinds of precious stone and metal. Six of these mountains form a range that encircles the seventh, which is much taller than the rest. This seventh mountain is God's throne from which He will pass out judgment on the souls gathered before Him during the Great Judgment.

At the base of the mountains are the Blessed and Accursed Places.

Constellation Correlations

As with some of the other spiritual locations mentioned in the Book of Enoch, the spiritual reality of the Fiery Mountain Range seems to have some correlation to a physical location on earth. Some believe the 7 stars to be the constellation Pleiades located above Antarctica which would be consistent with other ancient myths surrounding the constellation.

Blessed Place

Key Theme

- Eternal place where the merciful will bless the Lord, Who showed them mercy

Summary

The Blessed Place is the raised area before the throne of God that is filled with fragrant trees. At least one of these trees contains leaves/fruit that will cause supernaturally long life to those who eat from it[31].

Similar to the first of the Hollow Places, the Blessed Place is a serene environment where those who were merciful in life will be granted mercy by God. Jesus uses similar language to its description in the Book of Enoch in His Sermon on the Mount[32].

31 - Revelation 22:2

32 - Matthew 5:7

ACCURSED PLACE

Then the sixth angel blew his trumpet, and I heard a voice from the four horns of the golden altar before God, saying to the sixth angel who had the trumpet, "Release the four angels who are bound at the great river Euphrates." So the four angels, who had been prepared for the hour, the day, the month, and the year, were released to kill a third of mankind. The number of mounted troops was twice ten thousand times ten thousand; I heard their number.

John, the Apostle

Key Themes

- Eternal place for all accursed who speak against the Lord and His glory
- Burning fire
- Deep
- Destiny of the [evil] kings and the [evil] mighty
- Abyss of complete condemnation
- Rough Stones
- Imprisons the Watchers
- Has the mountains of gold, silver, iron, soft metal, and tin
- Has fiery molten metal and streams of fire that punishes angels
- Waters in that valley change temperature based on the state of the angels within it, and will heal the body as they punish the spirits

Summary

Similar in nature to the fourth of the Hollow Places, the Accursed Place (or Accursed Valley) lies among the mountains that make up the Fiery Mountain Range. The key difference between those who dwell in this valley and those who dwell in the fourth Hollow Place is that those in the Accursed Valley will, one day, be judged by God in that very spot[33].

The Accursed Valley is reserved as a place of judgment for the masses who were unrighteous, as well as the mighty men, kings, and even fallen Watchers that spoke and acted against God.

Scriptural Reference

While other locations feature either rough stone (usually for Watchers) or burning fire (usually for humans), this burning valley has both forms of punishment, for both forms of spirits. John's Revelation references this Valley and the angels that are imprisoned there[34].

The Water

A defining feature of the Burning Valley is the water that lies within it. While the language of 1 Enoch 67 is cryptic in regards to the waters, there are some defining characteristics. The waters have inverse effects in the spiritual and physical realms. While the waters may heal the body, their contents have a warping effect on the soul, driving it to lust. The Watchers that are imprisoned in this valley experience intense discomfort from these waters, and the temperature of the water will change depending on the state of the angels who share the space.

33 - It is possible (though not explicitly stated in any text) that the Blessed and Accused Places are used during the Great Judgment as the separate locations for the "sheep" and "goats" as described in John's Revelation. The Book of Enoch gives no timeline for this transfer of souls from the Hollow Places to the Blessed/Accursed Places, but given the details in John's Revelation the timeline might fit in this way - with the Hollow Places being a Pre-Great Judgment holding ground, and the Blessed/Accursed Places being the actual location of the Great Judgment event.

34 - Revelation 9:1-16

IMPLICATIONS OF THE HOLLOW PLACES

The concept of the existence of one or more temporary resting places before we reach our eternal home is not a new one - my Catholic brothers and sisters have been preaching this concept for centuries. However, the Hollow, Blessed, and Accursed Places paint a very different picture than the proclaimed Purgatory of the Catholic tradition. Their description also gives clarity to biblical passages that Evangelicals have been doing historical back flips in order to explain for generations.

If the Book of Enoch is going to be believed in the literal sense, then it asks the Bible student to view certain biblical passages in a different light than they may be accustomed to doing. Let's take three passages as examples.

The Raising of Samuel

In this less-than-Sunday-School-famous story, King Saul approaches a medium within his kingdom and asks of her one small thing: bring back the spirit of Samuel, the prophet, so that Saul can speak to him one more time. The witch complains, but ultimately complies with his request. Saul gets his meeting... much to the chagrin of the spirit of Samuel. Samuel spends the first of his precious moments back in the physical world rebuking Saul for disturbing his "rest." Interpreters explain this passage in various ways, though no additional context is given to invalidate the information given about the experience. Interestingly, the prophecy that Samuel does give (the death of Saul and his sons) ended up coming true.

Ancient Israel generally assumed a time of rest after death, followed by an eventual resurrection. Samuel would have thus been existing in this place of rest, presumably in the first of the Hollow Places.

The Rich Man and Lazarus

Scholars debate whether this story by Jesus was indeed merely a parable or a true story. The extra detail and the lack of typical parabolic structure lends itself to the truth of the story, but we aren't told its nature in the text. Either way, the story centers around a poor man (Lazarus) who dies and lies in rest with Abraham, and a rich man (unnamed) who dies and lies in torment. Jesus describes an uncrossable expanse between the two places, yet the two characters are apparently still able to see and communicate with one another. The descriptions of the two places are consistent with Hollow Places #1 and #2, with even the spring of water from the first Hollow Place being mentioned by Jesus.

The Thief on the Cross

The passage that most Evangelicals seem to lean on in argument against the Purgatory of the Catholic tradition is Jesus' promise to the thief on the cross that he would join him "today in Paradise." Evangelicals generally take this "Paradise" to mean "heaven," though the descriptions of the Blessed Place or first Hollow Place seem to fit more succinctly. It is unlikely that Jesus intended to imply that the thief would immediately find himself before streets of gold in Jesus' response, or he would have likely used a word that wasn't so closely associated with the themes that were already so rooted within the mind of the man dying next to him.

Conclusion

If the Book of Enoch is to be believed, then a great deal other passages would likely need revisiting in light of modern conceptualizations of the afterlife. While this prospect doesn't change the practical applications of the Gospel, its incorporation may require some adjustment of the language of its presentation.

MEMORANDUM 2: THE QUARTERS

Summary

The Book of Enoch describes the observable creation in four quadrants, or "quarters." To the east is the first quarter, rotating counter-clockwise directionally around a compass. Interestingly, in the southern quarter - the representation of earth - it was prophesied that the Most High would descend in "quite a special sense." And quite special, it was.

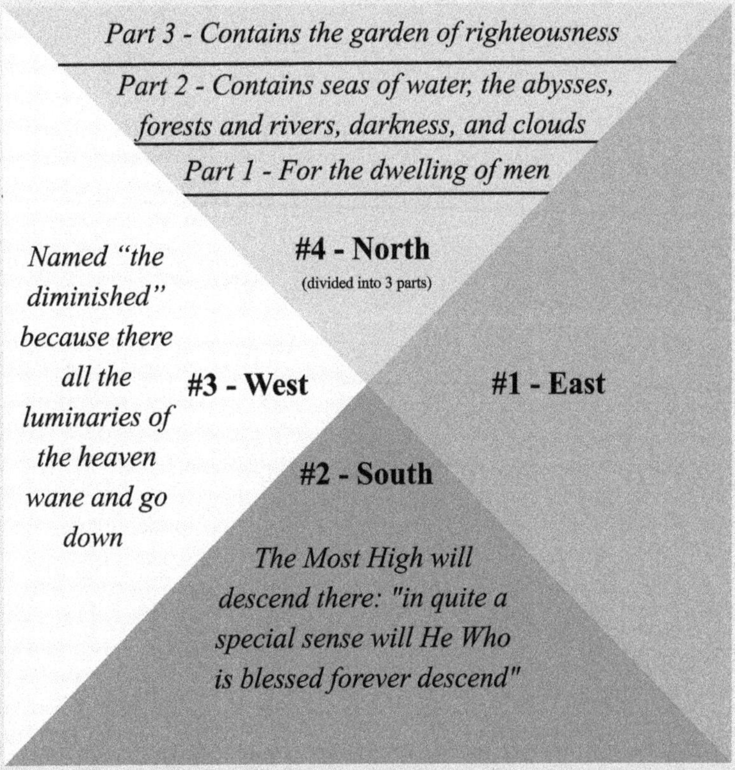

Part 3 - Contains the garden of righteousness

Part 2 - Contains seas of water, the abysses, forests and rivers, darkness, and clouds

Part 1 - For the dwelling of men

#4 - North

(divided into 3 parts)

Named "the diminished" because there all the luminaries of the heaven wane and go down

#3 - West

#1 - East

#2 - South

The Most High will descend there: "in quite a special sense will He Who is blessed forever descend"

Part 4: Delegates of the Seasons

Introduction to The Delegations of the Seasons

In the book of Enoch, each of the four seasons are said to be overseen by four groups of angelic servants numbering in the thousands, with one prominent angel to divide and have charge over the following group of 91 days.

Not all of these servants are listed, which seems to indicate that the specific naming of the custodians is not the key goal of the author.

Milki'el & Narel

Stations

Milki'el and Narel are the other leaders of the groups of 91 days. They are presumably over each of the colder seasons, though no record of the names of their sub-leaders is given.

MEL'EJAL

Station

Mel'ejal is the angel that is set over the 91 days of spring. He is also known as Melkeja or Tam'aini in various scripts. According to the Book of Enoch, during his dominion there is sweat, heat, calms, the trees bear fruit, leaves are produced on all the trees, the harvest of wheat and rose-flowers, flowers in the field, and the trees of winter become withered.

Mel'ejal has three angels who sub-lead under him, named Merka'el, Hilujaseph, and Zelebs'el who are each over roughly a month and a half of time.

HEL'EMMELEK

Station

Hel'emmelek is the angel that is set over the 91 days of summer. According to the Book of Enoch, during his dominion, there is glowing heat and dryness, trees ripen their fruits and produce all fruits ripe and ready, sheep pair and become pregnant, and the fruits of the earth are gathered.

Hel'emmelek has three angels who sub-lead under him, named Gida'ljal, Ke'el, and He'el who are each over roughly a month and a half of time. Asfa'el is the name of another of his sub-leaders, who is set over 1,000 other angels dedicated to this season. Though Asfa'el is the only head of 1,000 mentioned in the text, it is likely that each season has a relatively similar number of angels assigned to it.

WHY STUDY THE BOOK OF ENOCH?

Regardless of the original authorship or date of 1 Enoch, its cross-references by Jesus, Peter, Daniel, the author of Job, Jude, and debatably Moses all indicate that the work was widely accepted as authoritative - though not divinely inspired - especially in the second-temple period. Jude goes so far as to call some of the Book of Enoch "prophecy."

While the strict historical accuracy and the usefulness of a literal reading of the Book of Enoch is widely debated, the treatment of the text by the Prophets and Apostles leaves little doubt as to its usefulness in understanding the context into which the books of the Bible where written. For example, Leviticus 16 makes a reference to "Azazel," indicating that regardless of which *text* came first, the ancient Jews had a belief system associated with the Watchers well before the Law of Moses was recorded in the format that we possess today.

"Context is key." If one wants to better understand the context into which the books of the Bible were written, a thorough understanding of some of these preconceptions is vital in order to avoid inserting our own modern assumptions, into the text.

www.ingramcontent.com/pod-product-compliance
Ingram Content Group UK Ltd.
Pitfield, Milton Keynes, MK11 3LW, UK
UKHW062254290726
14090UKWH00017B/684